With Love from My Cat

by Georges Ware

aided by his cat, Nokomis

Includes notes on adopting and looking after your cat

Pen Press

First published in Great Britain by Pen Press

All paper used in the printing of this book has been made from wood grown in managed, sustainable forests.

ISBN13: 978-1-78003-158-3

Printed and bound in the UK
Pen Press is an imprint of
Indepenpress Publishing Limited
25 Eastern Place
Brighton
BN2 1GJ

A catalogue record of this book is available from the British Library

Cover design by Jacqueline Abromeit

With Love from My Cat

<u>Preface</u>

The author, Georges Ware BSc, MA, PhD, spent much of his life teaching and doing research at the University of Bristol, where his work was often associated with animals including mink and foxes. He was always careful to ensure that no harm ever came to these animals.

As a lifelong lover of cats he decided, on retiring, to build and run a boarding cattery which, for 20 years, has kept him in continuous contact with many people and their pets. The cattery is renowned for its exceptionally loving care and high standard of comfort, supervision and expertise.

Cats are not just pets. They can be really understanding friends with a remarkable ability to communicate with us. They provide wonderful company and comfort to the elderly and joy to younger folk. Many of the stories in this book centre on or around Christmas and more elderly people. Almost all were prompted either by Nokomis or other cats; others derive from real-life events. They may bring tears to your eyes but all have happy endings.

I am sometimes asked how cats can help one write stories; there are many ways. Several of the stories in this little book, for example *Precious*, *Pancho's Tale* and the *Broken Cat Flap*, are based on real-life events that I would never have known about had I not had a great involvement with cats. *The Arrival of Nokomis* in its latter part is an exact account of what actually happened that evening. In other instances the stories such as *Mr Bean* and *Was it a Miracle*, tell how cats can help us without either the cat or the person realising it. If you ever have to write a story about cats, or perhaps even about something else, just relax with a purring cat on your lap and listen to what he or she has to say. You may be surprised to find a story like *You Too Should Learn Cat-speak*, comes into your mind.

Over the years Georges and Ann have had many cats since Nokomis walked in. All have lived to a ripe old age and have always been replaced by cats housed by one of the cat charities and looking for a home or by a cat who, like Nokomis and Dylan, just walked in. Currently they have two cats, Alfie and Jeoffry, brothers aged 7, which were adopted from the *Cats Protection* 3 years ago.

Dr Ware records here his grateful thanks to his wife, Dr Ann Light, for her assistance in both the preparation of this book and the running of the cattery.

Jeoffry and Alfie

Nokomis Playing Chess

 ## The Arrival of Nokomis

Downward through the evening twilight,
In the days that are forgotten,
In the unremembered ages,
From the full moon fell Nokomis,
Fell the beautiful Nokomis.

(Henry Wadsworth Longfellow, 1855)

The little black and white kitten had been in her new home for only a few weeks. Life there was quite nice but not as lovely as when she'd been living with her mum in a big warm house with deep cosy carpets. In the old house she'd had a lovely basket which she shared with her brothers and mother, and the people in the house were gentle and kind, not only to the cats, but also to each other. In this new house many of the rooms had no carpets at all and she had to make do with an old cardboard box with newspapers in it for a bed. The food she was given was not as nice either and sometimes even seemed to be a bit smelly. But, as in her old home, there was a cat flap so she could

1

go into the garden, and that was something she was very grateful for because her new people seemed to quarrel a lot.

The man often started to shout at the lady and the lady always screamed back at him. Sometimes she even threw things at him. This frightened the little kitten so much that she had to rush out, through the cat flap, into the garden and hide under a bush at the far end and stay there until she felt it would be safe to return to the house.

One afternoon, things got even worse. The man came home rather late and seemed unable to walk straight, a quarrel started and the man hit the lady so hard that she fell on the floor. The poor kitten was terrified and rushed out into the garden. It was pouring with rain so she hid as best she could under her bush, watching the house, as usual, until it looked safe to go back indoors. But when she eventually plucked up courage to go back, she found the place deserted; no sounds at all and neither the man nor the lady was there.

She was very sad so curled up in her cardboard box and cried herself to sleep; there seemed no alternative.

Next morning, there was still no sign of anyone at home and she had to make do with some nasty old food that was left in her bowl and was rather dry. It was the same the next day, except that there was no food remaining for her at all, and the same again the day after and the day after that. Luckily, her mother had taught all the kittens how to catch mice and she spent much of that night chasing them in the garden, eventually catching a big fat one for a very late supper under her safe bush.

The next day a big lorry arrived at the house and took away all the furniture and carpets. The little kitten didn't know what to do, even her cardboard box had vanished. There seemed no point in staying in a cold house with no bed, no people, and no food, but where else could she go? She was very sad and very frightened so went to her special bush, lay down and, once more, cried herself to sleep.

She slept fitfully for most of the morning but it got very cold and white stuff, which she learnt later was called snow, started to fall from the sky and cover the ground. Her home beneath the bush was no longer the place to be, in fact, this house was no longer a home, so she went out through the back gate and onto the road wondering if, perhaps, she might find some nice house where kind people would look after her.

All day she walked the snow-covered streets, keeping safely to the pavements but only a few people noticed her.

'Oh! Look! What a sweet little kitten,' said one lady to another as they walked by. And a passing man commented, laughing that the kitten was right up to her tummy in snow. She came to one house which had a little front garden and a thick hedge, she made her way cautiously to front door as there was a slight smell of 'happy cat' on the path. She meowed loudly and waited but nothing happened so she walked round the side of the house looking for some way in. Suddenly a huge tabby cat appeared as if from nowhere and hissed fiercely at her, making her run for her life back to he roadway.

A long mile or so further on she saw another possible home and, even more cautiously this time, approached the front door and gave a meow.

To her surprise, the door opened almost immediately, and a lady stood looking at her with a large dog beside her.

'You can't come in here,' she said, giving the little cat a push with her foot. 'Rover would eat you!'

So the lonely little kitten had to go back to the road once again and continue her search, through the deep snow, for a new home. She was getting rather tired and very depressed, wondering if, perhaps, she should go back to her empty house, but at the same time knowing that she could never find her way back.

Better to go on, she thought, and continued her weary journey in the now evening twilight. A few more people stopped to stroke her or make silly little remarks to each other about her, but nobody offered her a home, or even a saucer of milk. And nobody at all noticed the tears in her eyes.

Nobody, that is, until late in the evening the next day, when it was quite dark and the full moon was shining brightly right overhead. Then, quite suddenly, she met an old lady pushing a little pram full of newspapers along the snow-covered pavement.

'Hello, little kitten,' she said, bending down to touch her. 'Are you lost?'

The kitten replied with a long sad meow that clearly voiced, 'Yes.'

'Come along with me and we'll find your home,' the lady said, thinking that the kitten lived locally. So they both continued along the road, the kitten running along anxiously behind the lady, who called at several houses to deliver newspapers. At each house the little cat stood beside her and looked longingly at the open door, but no one noticed her until they reached a house where the snow was very deep. So deep that the lady had difficulty getting the pram along the path. The little kitten's feet were now very cold and sore so, as soon as a man opened the door, she decided to risk all and slipped past the man and into the house without being noticed.

'Oh, I'm so glad she's found her home,' the old lady said, taking an evening newspaper from the pram and handing it to the man. He hadn't understood what she meant about 'finding her home', but returned with his newspaper to the living room where his wife, Ann, was sitting by the fire.

'Where did that kitten come from?' Ann asked, pointing to the little black and white cat now sitting on the hearthrug, washing its face and gazing into her eyes.

'No idea,' replied the man, suddenly understanding what the newspaper lady had meant. 'I think it must have slipped in through the front door just now. I wouldn't blame it, it's very cold out there and the snow is very deep, maybe it fell from the full moon,' he added jokingly.

Ann laughed and went to fetch a saucer of milk and then watched as the kitten lapped it up, trying to purr and drink at the same time. The kitten felt so grateful for that saucer of milk that she almost started to cry instead of purring.

'What shall we do with it?' Ann asked somewhat rhetorically, thinking at the same time that it was a very nice little cat and she had always loved cats.

'If we leave the back door ajar tonight, I expect it will find its way home,' her husband Georges suggested. But the little kitten felt very safe in that house and hoped so much that she would be allowed to stay. All three slept very well that night.

'It's still here!' Ann called to her husband on coming into the room the next morning. And when the couple got home from work that evening, happy meows and loud purrings from the little kitten, who was waiting in the hallway, greeted them.

'I think it wants to stay with us,' Ann said happily. 'What shall we call it?'

'Is it a boy or girl?' Georges asked, smiling in agreement to her suggestion and picking up the little cat to check.

'It's a girl,' he announced knowingly.

'We could call her Moonlight; it was a full moon last night.'

'Yes, perhaps, but that doesn't sound quite right. I have a better idea. Do you remember the story of Hiawatha?'

'Yes, a bit, we did the book at school. It was written by that chap Longfellow wasn't it? Why?'

'There was a girl who fell from the full moon, remember?'

'Yes, that's right, she was called Nokomis, wasn't she? *Daughter of the Moon, Nokomis.*'

'So let's call her Nokomis, it was a full moon when she came in and maybe she did fall from the moon – who knows?'

A few days later, as Nokomis was, of course, still in residence, Georges put a cat flap in their back door. Nokomis watched him carefully as he worked and she knew then, for certain, that she had at last found a new and loving home. To show her gratitude and that she knew about cat flaps, she immediately hopped out through it and then straight back in again. She was very happy and so very grateful. The couple loved their little cat very much and gave her lots of lovely food and a comfortable basket, lined with a real sheepskin rug.

It wasn't until much later that the couple realised that Nokomis could tell stories and would help them to write this little book.

You too should learn Cat-Speak

Elizabeth and Roger had two lovely cats, a tabby called Holmes and a ginger called Watson, who, like their namesakes, had very different characters. Holmes was a very talkative and adventurous cat, who regularly toured the neighbours' back gardens, often popping in through an open window, door or cat flap to receive a welcoming stroke and, sometimes, even a tasty little treat. And, of course, Holmes liked to keep a general eye on what was going on in the neighbourhood. Watson, on the other hand, being a typical ginger cat, preferred to spend the day curled up in his nice warm basket, purring away and dreaming about what he would do if he won the cat-lottery.

Elizabeth and Roger had been married for seven years, so Elizabeth was planning a celebration to mark their anniversary. She invited a couple of Roger's colleagues from work, John and Tracy from number 36, the young, newly-married couple from across the road, and Amanda, the pretty young doctor from number 40, with her boyfriend, plus a few of her friends from the sports club. Two retired elderly lady schoolteachers, who lived opposite, were also invited as they very kindly often came across to look after Holmes and Watson if Roger and Elizabeth had to be away for any reason.

As an anniversary present, Roger bought Elizabeth a pretty bracelet with little cat charms and she, after a lot of thought, bought for Roger a copy of the course on *Cat-speak*, researched and written by the famous cat psychologist, Professor Herman Freudenstein. She had seen it advertised by him extensively on QVC and it came as a boxed set with full dictionary, two CDs and an illustrated guide.

On the great day, the party turned out to be a marvellous success. Holmes was delighted to see all his friends and circulated among the guests rubbing himself against their legs and purring loudly. The lovely Amanda came alone, saying that she had given her boyfriend the push a week or so before. She was wearing a very pretty little skirt and black tights, and became an immediate star attraction for the boys, prompting Elizabeth to keep an extra eye on Roger. Watson, of course, took the opportunity to escape all the excitement and noise and had a good long sleep on his mistress's bed. At the end of the party, the two schoolteachers, who had drunk far too much, had to be escorted back across the road to their house, while Roger, as an act of chivalry, escorted Amanda home to her front door.

Elizabeth loved her bracelet and Roger amused himself with the course on cat-speak for a short while, but seemed not to have sufficient interest or time to study it properly. So, eventually, Elizabeth decided to take it over, much to the curiosity and amusement of both cats, as she practised the pronunciation of many meows and their associated vowel sounds.

Cat-speak is, however, a complex language. According to Freudenstein, cats can understand a lot of human speech but their own voice is limited to the production of what we casually describe as meows. The course points out right at the beginning that nearly all cat words start with the 'mi' sound but are then followed by sounds that cannot be represented by our normal alphabet. Freudenstien had, therefore, introduced a series of phonic characters representing other cat sounds. For example, as explained on the CDs, the sound for 'yes' in cat-speak is written as Miəəɲiɝfɡɡ and 'no' as MiXᴄ̧ᴄ̧aœ, whilst 'yes, please' and 'no, thanks' have œtɰʁ added without the preceding 'mi' sound. Lots of other words, such as breakfast – Miobŋɝ, lunch – MiɕXʋ, tea – Miʁtʁt, and supper – Minʤ**, are known to most cats but all sound almost identical to the uninitiated human and

11

are usually interpreted just as, 'I want food'. Many cats know a little about numbers too. Four, for example, is pronounced as Miəəi̵X.

It must have been a month or so after the party that Roger reported that the financial crunch was causing a lot of extra work at the office and that he would be quite often working late. Elizabeth naturally understood the importance of his job and, alone in the evenings, spent a lot of time doing the cat-speak course. Holmes, and even Watson, always watched and listened, with strange looks in their eyes, as she practised the sounds, and occasionally responded with odd comments, which, perhaps fortunately, she could not yet translate.

But as time passed, Roger seemed to be getting home later and later, sometimes not until after midnight. On one such occasion she was lying in bed reading her book for a change, while Watson slept soundly in his basket in the corner of the bedroom. Suddenly, Holmes came in noisily through the bedroom window, jumped onto the bed, cuddled up as usual beside Elizabeth and started to purr.

'Hello,' said Elizabeth, half asleep. 'I thought at first you were Roger.'

'MiX̧çaœ,' replied Holmes.

'Where is he do you think?' she asked rhetorically.

'Miǝ̈iⱠX Miʁⱱʁⱱ,' said Holmes clearly.

'Four tea?' questioned Elizabeth, delighted to be able to translate for once.

'Miǝ̈ɲiɜˤfgg,' responded Holmes positively and with a flick of his tail.

'Four tea?' Elizabeth questioned again.

'MiⱩ̧ç̧aœ Miǝ̈iⱠX Miʁⱱʁⱱ,' came Holmes's very positive reply, loudly and in a sort of, rather cross, treble meow.

Elizabeth pondered a while, looking questioningly at Holmes, then it struck her. 'Four tea', yes, of course, not 'four tea' but 'forty'. Roger was at number 40! Holmes had obviously popped in while on his nightly round and must have seen Roger there – supposedly working late! Vivid scenes of a cavorting Roger and Amanda went through Elizabeth's mind.

'Thank you, Holmes, you were well named,' she said, hastily getting dressed. 'We shall have to see about this.'

13

<u>In Praise of a Feral Cat</u>

Weep not I say for she who has no name
But share her joy! Admire her agile frame!
Somewhere, unknown to you, she has a bed,
Maybe beneath some old, discarded shed.
There in the warmth of love her kitts she'll raise
Purring to them her mother-song of praise.
In Nature's way she walks her daily path
Nearer to God than any by your hearth.

Precious

Precious!' she called, as soon as she returned home from shopping. 'Precious?' She had bought a special pack of cat treats from the corner shop and wanted Precious to have some straight away, but there was no response. He had obviously gone out into the garden and not heard her return. She was fully aware of the vagaries of cats' hearing; it wasn't usually that they couldn't hear, but more often that they didn't want to hear. Her cat, she knew, could hear a mouse move 100 yards away, but only if he wanted to.

Precious had turned up in her garden soon after she had moved into this new, smaller house after retiring and he had clearly been in need of a home. Of course, she had at once fallen in love with the little cat, which provided her with such good company, and had immediately decided to call him Precious. Since then, eight years of happy and mutually-rewarding friendship had passed.

'Precious?' she called again going to the back door and looking briefly into the garden, but again there was no response. But cats will be cats and wander off, from time to time, on their routine cat business and so she was not unduly worried.

She called him again just before sitting down to the little lunch that Meals on Wheels had brought her. Today it was roast lamb in gravy with peas and mashed potato with a jam tart to follow, but still Precious did not appear, which surprised her as he nearly always came to see what she was having for lunch and to enjoy any leftovers. She didn't feel like much lunch, and after she had eaten what she could, she called again for Precious, but there was still no sign of him.

That afternoon she had an unexpected visitor; a neighbour from further up the cul-de-sac, who occasionally dropped in to see how she was and perhaps stay and play a game or two of Scrabble. This time she had brought with her a small box of chocolates and two home-made cakes. Because she was old and lived alone, the neighbours were very kind to her.

'Where's Precious today?' her visitor asked.

'Oh, he's being a bad boy and hasn't been home since breakfast time.'

'That's strange, I think this must be the first time I've called and he hasn't been sitting in his favourite chair by the window. I do hope he's all right.'

'Oh, I'm sure he's just up to some mischief, it's not as though we live on a busy road where he could get run over. He often wanders over the garden wall and into those allotments; I expect there are lots of mice and things there.' But in her own mind she was troubled.

Her visitor left after they had played two games and enjoyed a nice tea together. She said she hoped Precious would be home soon.

'Do let me know if there's anything you want at anytime, won't you,' she said, as she always did, and left for home.

Tea-time came, and eventually supper-time, for which the old lady boiled herself an egg. She wasn't feeling like food at all. Rather later than usual, after watching the ten o'clock news on her reliable old television, she went up to bed, but there was still no sign of her cat. She slept badly that night, waking at every little sound and wondering if it was the cat flap and expecting, or rather hoping, that Precious would jump onto her bed moments later. But morning came, and still absolutely no sign of him. Even before she made herself a cup of tea, she went out into the garden, wearing only her dressing gown over her nightdress, to call for Precious. She walked the whole length of the garden and peered over the wall to see if she could see him in the allotments beyond the garden but, to her dismay, there was no sign or sound of her dear cat.

After dressing, she made herself a little breakfast of toast and tea but found that she really had no appetite, so left it on the table and went out into the road to look for Precious. She walked the 100 yards down to the junction with the main road, crossed over and walked back up the other side. All the way she called for Precious and peered into the gardens she passed hoping to see him, but also fearing she might see his dead body on the street. She walked past her house and on up towards her special friend. There she stopped, hesitated for a moment, and then knocked on the door.

'Hello! What a surprise! Do come in.'

'Precious hasn't come home.' Her friend thought she could see tears in her eyes as she spoke.

'He's only been gone for a day and a night, cats often do that,' she said as reassuringly as she could. 'Has he never been away for a night before?'

'No, never overnight.'

'Well, no need to worry yet, give him a day or two more,' she encouraged but secretly, knowing how much the old lady loved him, started to worry herself about what might have happened to the cat.

'Look, I'm going into town this morning, how would you like to come with me in the car?'

She pondered this question, realising that to go with her friend would be a lovely outing, but suppose Precious came home and she wasn't there to welcome him? But, after a little persuasion, said she would love to come as she did have some Christmas shopping still to do.

'But I must go home and put on some other shoes first,' she said, meaning really that she wanted to check that Precious had not come home while she had been out.

They enjoyed their visit to town as much as they could; there were so many shops and always so much more choice at the big supermarket than at the corner shop. Her friend was reassured to notice that she bought, among other things, some very special tins of cat food.

The afternoon passed with no sign of Precious and again she hardly slept at all that night, listening all the while for the click-clack of the cat flap or a happy meow as Precious came into her bedroom. But, sadly, there were no such sounds that night.

Next day there was still no sign of Precious and she went, again, to call on her friend.

'He's not back,' she said, now unashamedly with tears running down her cheeks. 'What should I do?'

Her friend suggested they phone the local vet, but he said that he had not seen Precious and that nobody had brought in an injured cat. Then they rang the police, who also said there had been no reports of stray cats but, nevertheless, made detailed notes of the cat's description and promised to phone if they received any information. The RSPCA also took detailed notes and promised to phone if they had news of Precious. Finally, they tried the local cat sanctuary. Though they had not seen him, they were very concerned and told her that she should not worry too much as cats, particularly male cats, did sometimes go off for long explorations of the neighbourhood.

Of course, she had all this while kept Precious's feeding tray in the kitchen topped up with fresh milk and food, however distressing it had been to throw away the uneaten meals. But today, the fifth day that Precious had not been seen, she decided that she was being silly. She must face the truth, Precious was gone, would never come home again and she might never know what had happened to him. So she cleared away the feeding tray, washed his little dishes and put them away in the cupboard. Then, with tears filling her eyes and running down her cheeks, she fetched his basket from its place by the living room hearth and put it away in the attic. Precious was gone.

The next day was Christmas Eve and she had earlier made plans with her friend to go to the midnight carol service in the cathedral. She had been every year of her life since she was 15, except one year when, as a teenager, she had had measles. She wondered if Precious, looking down from cat heaven, would mind her going but was sure he would not want her grief for him to prevent her going out on this very special evening. So, when her friend rang saying she would pick her up at 10:30 the next evening, she said that, yes, in spite of her grief, she would come to the service as it might give her the strength she would need to go on without him.

The cathedral looked beautiful with hundreds of candles lighting the nave. They chose two seats close to the front and sat listening to the organ for a few minutes. Then the choir started to process down the aisle with the leading chorister singing, solo, the opening verse of *Once in Royal David's City*. It was all so like it always was, except that there was now something missing in her life, which made her lips tremble as she tried to sing. They sang all her favourite carols and she listened once again to the telling of the Christmas story. The short sermon with the importance of love and friendship as its theme made her think, yet again, of her love and loss of Precious and she said a little prayer for him. As they left, the cathedral clock struck one; it was one o'clock on Christmas morning. Her friend drove her home but declined her invitation to a cup of cocoa.

'It's rather late,' she said, 'I really ought to get back; I have a lot to do in the morning.'

They waved goodbye and her friend drove off as she unlocked the front door. She tried hard not to look for anything special in the hallway as she knew, deep down, there would be nothing there and made her way to the kitchen. She made herself a cup of cocoa, and took two digestive biscuits from the tin and then, slowly climbing the stairs, made her way towards her lonely little bedroom. Even before she switched on the light, she saw a lump on the bed. Could it be? No, of course it couldn't, not after all this time. She switched on the light.

'Oh, Precious!' she called out, tears of joy running immediately from her tired eyes. 'Oh, Precious, where have you been?'

But Precious wasn't telling. He stood up and his loud, complaining meow said clearly: 'Where's my supper?'

The National Cat Show

The National Cat Show was terribly grand,
With cats there of all shapes and sizes.
The judges, too, were a very posh lot
As they summed up the cats and gave prizes.
But there wasn't a cat in that very great show
That seemed half as worthy as my moggy, Joe.

Joe is a rather aggressive old cat
Which is proved by the state of his ears.
They are frayed at the edges, his nose too is scarred,
Which earns him respect from his peers.
But there wasn't a cat in that very great show
That looked half as brave as my moggy, Joe.

The Asians had coats which were short and compact.
The Persians had fur that was silky.
There were spotteds and tabbies and bi-colours too
And 'creams' that, in truth, were more 'milky'.
But there wasn't a cat in that very great show
With fur half as thick as my moggy, Joe.

Some breeds were said to be terribly rare
And some were worth hundreds of pounds.
They must sleep on cushions embroidered with gold
In houses where money abounds.
But there wasn't a cat in that very great show
That I'd think of swapping for my moggy, Joe.

One winning cat's eyes were the deepest of blue.
An Asian had eyes that looked mean.
There were white cats with each eye a different hue!
One black's were the brightest of green.
But there wasn't a cat in that very great show
With eyes half as loving as my moggy, Joe.

Pancho's Tale

Once upon a time, a young, all-black tomcat called Pancho lived on one of those lovely sunny Spanish islands. He had no home and was free to roam the district and catch mice, of which there were plenty about, for his dinner. But one cold winter's day – they do have cold, wet winter days, even on those islands – Pancho wandered into one of the many local holiday hotels in search of shelter. There he found quite a few other cats, all being well cared for, and, which was very important to Pancho, there were plenty of delicious leftovers from the hotel guests' dinner tables for the cats' suppers.

Pancho was delighted with this discovery and decided that this new life was to be preferred to his rather lonely existence in the wild. So he settled down and made friends with some other cats, with the barmaid, and with many of the hotel guests, some of whom he noticed came back from time to time, recognised him at each visit, and sometimes brought him very special treats from home.

Many months passed by happily until, one day, a new manager arrived at the hotel and took over all responsibility, not only for the guests but also for the several resident cats, including Pancho. But the new manager didn't like cats. He said they made messes around the hotel, worried some of the guests, and that the bar smelt of tomcat, so *something would have to be done.*

He first talked to the local vet about having all the cats put to sleep, but luckily for Pancho and the other cats, the vet emphatically refused, saying that such a dramatic solution to his problem was not only immoral but actually against the Spanish law.

So the new manager had to have another think. Eventually he decided to build a large wire enclosure where all the cats would live. They would be well looked after but not be allowed to escape from the cage and so would not be a nuisance to him. Suddenly therefore, Pancho found himself virtually in prison. He went carefully all round the cage looking for a way out into the hotel's lovely garden, but there was none. He felt very sad and just curled up under a little tree and cried.

Many sad weeks followed during which he could not wander round the swimming pool, talk to the guests, get the odd cuddle, and catch the occasional mouse. Even the food the manager sent to the cage was not as nice as the food they had all had before. Poor Pancho got very thin and his fur started to fall out, leaving bald patches, and he wondered and wondered what to do. How could he and the other poor cats escape and would their torment ever end? Pancho was very sad indeed. But one day, just as he had given up all hope of any happiness ever again, one of the regular visitors to the hotel, who loved cats dearly, came along to the cage and called, 'Pancho?'

Pancho ran quickly to the wire and meowed loudly.

'Can't you come out for a cuddle?'

Pancho, understanding every word, shook his head and gave one little whining meow.

That's awful! the guest thought and walked round the cage, followed by Pancho, and looking to see if there was any kind of door, but the only one was locked with a heavy iron chain.

That evening the guest had a word with the manager, but was told firmly that the confinement of the cats was absolutely essential for the proper running of a top-class establishment like his and that no exceptions could be made. The guest was deeply distressed and decided that *something would have to be done*.

By a strange coincidence, someone, by moonlight that night, managed to cut a small hole in the wire while Pancho and the others watched excitedly. Pancho was the first to scramble though the hole, followed by the others, and leapt joyfully into the saviour's arms, purring loudly. But after a long cuddle, Pancho jumped down and made off, together with all the other cats, to the safety of the surrounding grounds.

Next day, Pancho came back just once to say farewell to the special guest, but, after that, was seen no more – at least no more at that time.

It wasn't until Pancho's special guest returned to the hotel a year later and was wandering along the seashore one evening, thinking about Pancho and wondering where he was and if he was all right, that there was a suddenly a loud meow. There was Pancho, sitting on a mound, close to a lovely house, gazing at the moon.

'Pancho!' the guest called, delighted to see him. Pancho turned, smiling as only a cat can, winked and waved a joyful tail, sending a loud purr wafting though the warm night air but he didn't move an inch. His friend understood why because beside him sat a lovely lady-cat and two beautiful kittens.

The Joy of Kittens

I wake to mewings on the bed,
My eyelids feel like lumps of lead.
I think the clock says ten past three
And then I fully wake to see
It's kitten-time! It's kitten-time!
Oh, happy, happy kitten-time.

By morning's light I counted four,
All firmly held by Mother's paw,
And reassuring purrings tell
That Mum and kits are doing well.
It's kitten-time! It's kitten-time!
Oh, most endearing kitten-time.

It's two weeks now and opened eyes
Survey the world in mild surprise.
And what a joy it is to know
That they can love each other so.
It's kitten-time! It's kitten-time!
Oh, most rewarding kitten-time.

By six weeks old, they're on the beds,
The curtain bottoms torn to shreds.
While Mum eats two whole tins a day
And I'm the one who has to pay!
It's kitten-time! It's kitten-time!
Oh, most expensive kitten-time.

Two months now passed, and all too soon,
The kittens leave this afternoon.
I know that Mum and I will cry
The moment we have said 'good-bye'.
That's kitten-time! That's kitten-time!
The saddest, saddest kitten-time.

But though the people came by car,
We know they've not gone very far,
And every Mum must surely know
Their little ones will one day go.
And we both heard the people say
'Oh, happy, happy kitten-day!'

Nokomis and kittens

No problem

The bank manager had tried to explain to her how she had lost nearly all her money, but she couldn't really understand how someone working in a financial office on the other side of the world could rob her of her life's savings and her home, just like that. The social worker had been kindness itself. She also had done her best to explain the collapse of the international finance company and, what was more important, had found her a nice little room in an old peoples' home on the other side of town.

'We'll move you after Christmas and you can bring some of your personal things along with you,' she explained, adding, 'but we'll have to get rid of that cat.'

'That cat', the expression had really hurt. She wasn't worried about herself; she could, she thought, manage on the social security money – just – and, perhaps her house really was getting a little too big for just her and String. They had called the cat String because, when the tiny, cold

35

and wet kitten had walked in shortly before her husband had died, it had had a long piece of string tied round its neck. So String had been her companion and friend for nearly ten years and she worried now more about him than about anything else. But it was Friday and, as she did every Friday, she walked to Mr Patel's corner shop to buy a little weekend treat for herself and for String; this week she chose a pot of salmon pâté. While in the shop, she picked up a lottery card, as she did most weeks, so that she could spend the evening deciding on her choice of lucky numbers and discuss with String how they would spend the winnings.

Later, that afternoon, with String purring on her lap, she tried to concentrate on her library book, but sad thoughts of the new little room and life without String kept entering her mind. What would 'they' do with him and where would he be, she wondered, speaking softly to String. She had read about cats that walked miles to find their homes. Would String ever find that one special little window behind which she would be waiting for him? She thought of him trudging the cold wet streets, endlessly searching for her, and a tear trickled down her cheek. String noticed and raised his paw to her face as if to dry it away.

'I won't let them take you away,' she promised him and he purred. She knew he had understood.

Trying to pull herself together, she picked up her book again. A large tear-and-powder-stained paw print graced the centre of the page and she worried for a moment that the librarian would notice it and scold her.

But four big toes on page thirty-four? Well, why not? she thought, taking the lottery card from her bag. Cats sometimes knew things that we didn't, and she marked off the two numbers, four and thirty-four. String seemed to smile up at her with his big amber eyes.

That evening, String watched expectantly as she prepared a late supper tray, including the little plastic tub of salmon pâté. Then, sitting in her favourite chair with the tray on her knees, she put the lid of the tub, well covered with salmon, on the floor for String. He lapped it up quickly, licking the lid completely clean all the while pushing it towards her foot and then meowed loudly. She bent down to put a second helping of pâté on the lid, but String had turned it over and was pressing it tighter and tighter against her foot. On the lid, 'Best Before 29/12' stood out boldly. She stroked String, added a big spoonful of pâté to the lid and took out her lottery card. Again String seemed to smile and purred loudly.

Of course, String always slept on her bed, and this night was to be no exception. In the morning she was woken by him knocking her spectacle case off the chest of drawers. It had been a long time since he had climbed up there. As a kitten he had regularly done so to reach the swinging pendulum of the old cuckoo clock, which, although it had lost its 'cuckoo' long ago, nevertheless, still kept excellent time.

For a long time, String watched the pendulum intently, just as he used to. Then, as she watched, he suddenly raised one paw, stopped the swinging pendulum and meowed excitedly. Seven thirty-one. Were these String's choice for her last two numbers? To String's obvious delight, she once more took the lottery card from her bag on the bedside table.

As always, straight after breakfast on Saturday morning, she went along to Mr Patel's and handed him her completed lottery card and the necessary payment, at the same time worrying that she might be wasting her now limited funds. But she had promised String. Mr Patel smiled broadly, wished her luck and handed back the certified card. That evening whilst watching television, String sat on her lap, purring more and more loudly as the brightly coloured balls rolled from the lottery machine.

Neither she nor String ever told anyone exactly how much they won that evening, but the bank manager said that she would be able stay on in her house with String.

'No problem,' he said.

Salmon Pate
Best before
29/12

To an Old Stray Cat

You were old, dear Cat, when you came to my door
And dirty and hungry and lame.
You were so scared of people you wouldn't come near
You'd no home and no hope and no name.

So I made you a house at the back of the yard,
It was only an old cardboard box,
And in it a bed lined with polythene bags
With blankets of old shirts and socks.

With lots of good grub, your warm bed and care,
You were soon well and strong as could be,
And though you went back to your life in the wild
You sometimes came back for your tea.

As years came and went, you learned I'd not bite
And allowed me to stroke you a little,
So now, when it's cold, you sometimes creep in
And curl up, by my fire, on the settle.

But it can't be long now till you leave me for good,
I pray that you'll suffer no pain,
And hope that you die on the warmth of my bed
And not somewhere outside in the rain.

Old Mr Bean

Mr Bean had no friends these days. They used to have lots but they had been mostly his wife's and when she died he had moved to the little cottage, just outside town, where he knew no one. He was only 65 but had always been known as Old Bean which annoyed him but was, he felt, better than being called Beano as he was at school.

Conscious of his loneliness, the lady in the local paper shop asked him, 'Why don't you get a dog to keep you company? He would be a good friend for you.'

'I don't like dogs,' said Mr Bean sharply. He had once, as a child, been mildly bitten by one, which had put him off dogs.

'Well, how about a cat then?' she suggested.

'I don't really like cats either,' he responded, picking up the change she was holding out for him and leaving the shop.

That night in his lonely little bedroom, before dozing off, he wondered whether it might, after all, be rather nice to have a cat purring away at his side, so next day he bought a copy of the local evening paper and looked at the small ads. Yes, there were several on offer, but all expensive pedigrees costing £250 or more and he didn't want to spend that kind of money on something he wasn't really sure about.

Mr Bean went back to the village shop, as usual, next day and confronted the lady.

'I've been thinking about your advice,' he said, 'and wondered if you had any idea where I could get an ordinary cat; the ones in the paper are all pedigrees.'

The lady smiled broadly. 'I have a friend who might have one,' she said, writing down the name and address of the friend for him.

Mr Bean thanked her and said he would go straight round to see her. Half an hour later, the cat lady was showing him a little black cat that had been abandoned and needed a home, but she didn't, of course, know its name.

So, that evening, Mr Bean found himself sitting by the log fire in the cottage with a very grateful cat sitting on his lap purring loudly. He had to admit that he did feel a little happier. He wondered what to call him and, having a great sense of humour, decided to name the little cat Heinz. It wasn't long before they became real friends and learned some of the secrets of cat-speak, but still, quite often Mr Bean felt that the little cat didn't really fill the big lonely gap in his life. Heinz was also conscious of the occasional sadness in the air but didn't know what he could do to help more.

It was some days later that Mr Bean felt that Heinz deserved a little present, so he went round to the local pet shop, which he had obviously never entered before, and spent quite a long time looking round the various little luxuries that he thought Heinz would appreciate. Eventually he chose a little woolly bed and took it along to the counter handing the bed and his credit card to the shop lady. She looked at the card carefully before inserting it into the card reader. 'James Bean', she read and her mind clicked.

'Excuse my asking,' she said, 'but I don't suppose your wife is called Shirley is she, used to be Shirley Blake?' Mr Bean looked at her in amazement.

'How did you know that?' he asked.

'Oh, my name is Sarah, we used to be great friends in the old days, I shall never forget the day she told us she was to become Mrs Bean. We all thought that was terribly funny. Oh! I'm sorry that was a bit cheeky of me, but how is Shirley?'

'Alas I'm afraid she died a while ago, I'm all alone now, but I do remember her mentioning you. Didn't you both go to art classes or something?'

'Oh, that is sad,' the shop lady said. 'Yes, you are right we did go to art classes and I still do every Wednesday afternoon, I find them very relaxing and rewarding. You must come round to supper one evening and meet my husband, Jim; how about Tuesday, shall we say seven o'clock?'

'That is so kind of you,' Mr Bean replied feeling genuinely grateful for the invitation. 'I shall look forward to it.'

The supper was a great success, Sarah showed Mr Bean some of her paintings and there was one, very old and not very good, of Shirley sitting by her easel at the art class. Sarah also managed to persuade Mr Bean to join the classes with her and Jim, telling him that he would soon become quite a good artist. Heinz noted that his master seemed happier over the next few weeks and when Shirley and Jim came to supper one night he realised why. His master had new friends!

It wasn't long after that that Heinz started coughing a lot. So Mr Bean immediately made an appointment with the local vet and, after sitting for quite a long time in the vet's waiting room with Heinz in a cardboard box with holes in it on his lap, he was called into the consulting room. The vet held out his hand, as he always did to welcome the new client, but suddenly stopped, looked curiously at Mr Bean and shouted, 'Beano!'

Mr Bean immediately recognised his old school friend. 'Mike old chap, I had no idea you lived round here. How are you?'

After quite a long chat, the vet got round to having a good look at Heinz.

'Nothing serious,' he commented with a chuckle about the name. 'Cats do rather fuss at the slightest discomfort. I think he has a mild chill that will put itself right in a day or two. But you must come round and meet my wife one evening.' Mike got out his diary.

'How about Monday for dinner? Shall we say seven o'clock?'

'Thank you, that will be lovely.'

When they got home Heinz seemed better already. It's strange how often a visit to the vet seems to be an immediate cure for cats!

Mr Bean enjoyed the dinner immensely. Not only was the food superb but he and Mike had a wonderful session reminiscing about their school days, while Mike's wife did the washing up. Before leaving, Mr Bean was delighted to be able to arrange a return evening, which greatly pleased Heinz and made him purr more loudly than Mr Bean had ever hear him purr before.

Over the following months, Mr Bean started to play golf with his veterinary friend and also became quite a good artist in watercolours. He also met at art class a rather attractive lady who had been recently widowed and had also just taken up golf and painting. She seemed to get on immensely well with Mr Bean and immediately fell in love with Heinz. You can, I'm sure, guess the very happy end to this story, and all because of a little black cat!

Credit Card

3434 5812 4456 3758

Exp: 25/12/2015

James Bean

Musty's Big Fright

Musty was just eight months old. He and his two little sisters had been born at the end of summer in a lovely country house, but his life so far seemed to have been filled with various ups and downs. How well he remembered that night about six weeks ago, when there were suddenly lots of loud bangs and sparks all over the sky and a great big blazing fire in the garden. His mother had been a little scared too and had taken them all into the back room.

There had been other bad times too, but now at last, he was living in a warm house with kind people. They fed him the best food and they had two nice young children who loved to play with him and who also let him sleep in peace when he was tired. At this particular moment he was lying, half asleep, on the rug by the fire thinking about some of those days gone by.

He could remember his mother, a big tabby cat, and the way he and his sisters used to lie curled up beside her enjoying a long drink of her warm tasty milk. She had taught them how to wash themselves, how and where to go to the toilet, and how to catch things to eat, just in case they ever found themselves hungry. In the first lessons, they caught several kinds of creepy-crawlies which didn't really taste very nice, but later Mother took them out into the garden where they learned not only to climb trees but to catch bigger things, and one day they caught a mouse. Then sadly, one morning just as they all seemed to be enjoying growing up, a lady called with a basket and took away his two sisters. After they had gone, the house seemed very lonely and he now had no one but Mother to play with and even she seemed to be less inclined to play.

Days passed and Mum seemed to grow ever less friendly to him, occasionally even hissing at him when he came to her and asked for milk, and once she even biffed him on the nose with her big paw. Musty began to wonder what would happen to him and then, quite without any warning, he too was popped into a basket and taken on a noisy, bumpy journey to a place where he was put in a tiny room with iron bars like a cage, all by himself. There was no other cat in the cage-room to talk to and the lady who came to feed him twice a day never seemed to have any time to stroke him or to give him a real cuddle. She did, however, give him a good rub down with a stiff brush once a week, which was nice, though it sometimes hurt him a bit. He was never allowed out and had to use a tiny box, filled with white stuff, as his toilet. Time and more time passed very slowly, now and then people would come and look at him through the bars and then go away. Naturally poor Musty had no idea why he was in this cold unfriendly place, nor when or if ever, he might see his mother, sisters or anyone he knew again.

Then, at last on one afternoon, a family passed by his little prison.

'Oh, Mummy,' cried the little girl of the family. 'Look at that little black and white one. Isn't she lovely?'

Musty ran to the bars, meowed loudly and looked straight into the little girl's eyes pleading to be taken away from this horrible, lonely place.

'Yes, Mummy, I like her too!' added the boy. 'Can we have her?'

The lady who fed Musty came along to the group and they asked her about Musty. She explained that Musty's original name was Moustache because of the patch of white fur beneath his nose. He was a boy cat and he had been neutered, whatever that meant, and yes, they could have him and would they like to hold him for a bit to make sure?

Mummy said yes, they would like to see if Musty was gentle and friendly. Of course, Musty heard this and put on his very best and most loving behaviour as he was passed round the family, purring as he was stroked and cuddled, as black and white cats always do, and finishing up in Dad's arms.

'Yes, we will take her please,' said Daddy finally.

'Him,' corrected the feeding lady, promptly pushing Musty into a cardboard box and closing the lid so it was all dark and he could not see out at all.

After another long, dark, bumpy and frightening journey, Musty found himself in a nice room with a big hearthrug and a warm glowing fire – just like the one he had known with his Mummy. The family were watching him closely.

'Here's a nice bowl of milk for you,' said the daughter, placing it beside the fire.

Musty was delighted; he'd had no milk since leaving his home as the feeding lady gave him only water, and soon after that, the girl's mother came in with a big plateful of chicken!

Musty didn't feel very hungry at that moment. He was too eager to explore the house and see if there was a garden like there had been at his old home. First he went all round the room looking under the chairs and tables, then he found the stairs and explored the bedrooms, and lastly the kitchen where he noticed a cat flap like the one his mother had taught him how to open. He tried pushing the flap, first with a paw and then with his nose, but it would not open.

'You can't go out yet, Musty,' came the little boy's voice behind him. 'The lady said that we must keep you in for three weeks before you can go out because you might run away.'

Now, why ever would I do that? thought Musty, without saying even a little meow.

He found a litter tray in the corner of the kitchen, just like the one that he had in the cage-room and decided to test it, which seemed to please the family who were still watching his every move. Musty felt suddenly very tired, it had been quite a day! So he curled up in the little basket that the people had put down for him, in a corner by the fire and went into a deep, purring sleep.

Next morning he heard the lady calling him from the kitchen and found breakfast waiting for him. When he had eaten three quarters of it, he noticed the lady open the kitchen door and go into the garden to shake a duster. Musty seized the opportunity to slip past her and ran into the garden.

'Musty! Come back! Come back!' came the lady's voice. But Musty wanted very much to explore first. He had no intention of leaving the lovely new home or of getting lost! He gazed up at the several trees, explored some gooseberry bushes and scratched around on the grass lawn, eventually choosing an area of the cabbage patch to dig a real hole. Then he headed back to the kitchen door, where the lady was waiting for him, but he did not go in. Instead, he scratched at the cat flap and, just as he had hoped, she opened it for him. So now, at last, he had a real home and the key to the door!

Musty loved his basket in the corner by the fire. It was his place and no one ever disturbed him there. No one, that is, until one terrible night.

The first sign that something was wrong had been when Musty came in from the garden and saw a large tree, growing in the corner of the room, right next to his basket. He approached it very cautiously, as he had never seen a tree growing in a room before. What would happen if a whole forest of trees sprang up in all the rooms, Musty wondered. He looked more carefully, and found that the tree was surrounded by earth in a big pot.

Ah! It's a new kind of litter box! Musty concluded and climbed onto the big pot. But there seemed to be no space for him to squat on the pot so that couldn't, after all, be what it was for. Over the next couple of days the children hung some shiny red, blue and silver balls on the branches and put some boxes, wrapped in coloured paper round the big pot. Musty was puzzled and a little scared so decided it would be safest to give up his basket and move to a chair on the far side of the room.

He was fast asleep a night or two later when he was woken by an awful noise in the fireplace and, without any warning, there was a man, just visible in the dark room, standing by the tree. He was wearing a long red coat and red hat with a white bobble on top. His mother had warned him to keep well away from strange men so he fled to safety under the sofa and watched the man hang some more little things on the tree. Then, as suddenly as he had appeared, the man in the red coat vanished, leaving only a strong smell which Musty thought was rather like the smell of the horses at his old country home. Musty stayed in the safety of the sofa until the family came down the next morning.

The children seemed overjoyed by the tree and especially by the extra little things left by the man in the red coat.

'Musty, come out from under the sofa and see what Santa has brought you,' they called.

Musty approached cautiously and they pointed to one little parcel on the bottom branch with 'For Musty' written on it. Musty stretched up and pulled it off the tree with his claws and tore off the coloured paper wrapping. It contained a little woollen mouse which smelt strongly of some wonderful stuff that grew in his old garden. He tossed it in the air several times, catching it each time, and eventually carried it off to his basket so he could enjoy its smell as he slept.

Musty was thrilled with his present and decided never to be frightened by trees in the house or by the man in the red coat called Santa, should he ever call again. He felt so happy to have such a lovely safe home again and there was no longer any need to worry about being told off by his mum.

An Old Man's Prayer for his Cat

So many years ago she came to me,
A trusting tiny ball of fluff
That climbed my leg to play
And sleep upon my lap.
For all those years, and still,
We shared our joys and love,
But now are both grown old
And, soon, must die.
Her eyes, like mine, are clouded now.
If I went first,
She could no longer see to catch her prey.
Nor could she understand the missing saucer,
Cold hearth and empty bed.
Nor bend her ways to suit some stranger's house.

Pray, take her first, O Lord,
That I may see her resting, safe,
Deep beneath the apple tree that once
She loved to climb
With such agility, far beyond my reach.
I shall grieve with understanding,
Then anyone can bury me.

Was it a Miracle?

'You can't keep it, you know. Not with those legs of yours.' The district nurse was adamant as she busied herself preparing to give the old lady's legs their daily massage.

The old lady wasn't really that old; it was just her legs. They had been left numb and useless by a bad fall a year ago. The doctor had said they might get better, but so far they had not.

'No, there's certainly no way you could keep a cat. Besides, they bring disease and their saucers breed flies,' the district nurse added with distaste.

Everyone seemed to be against it. The little cat had come in from the cold a few weeks before Christmas and had slept on her bed every night. The lady from Meals on Wheels had told her that they could certainly not bring food for it and that it would have to go, and the social worker had even telephoned the council's dog warden to come and take it away. But when he came, the old lady, sitting in her chair, had hidden the little cat under her long tweed skirt.

She did wish they would let her keep the little cat. She had so longed for one, but the animal rescue charities had all refused to let her have one of their strays because of her legs. The old lady understood how difficult it would be. Even now the little cat was meowing at the empty saucer that the social worker had, grudgingly, filled with milk for it. She raised her long skirts and patted her legs, trying to show the little cat that it was no good and that she could not easily walk to get milk. The little cat ran to her feet, stopped and looking at one leg, playfully sank its claws into her shin.

The numb legs felt nothing at first, but as the little cat continued to sharpen its claws on her leg, she cried out in pain. The little cat looked up, paused for a moment, then climbed slowly and painfully up the other leg and snuggled into her lap.

The old lady was surprised by the pain, it was something she had not felt since the paralysis had set in and as it passed, she felt a new warmth creeping down both legs. Some feeling in them seemed to have suddenly returned and she wondered if she could perhaps now even move them and made as if to do so. But, as she had half feared, nothing happened so she sank back in her chair comforted, at least a little, by their new-found warmth.

A short while later the little cat went again to the saucer, meowing yet more insistently for milk, but again the old lady could only point to her legs.

Again the little cat came and sat on her feet. She felt its weight and thought she felt her toes move in the slippers, she tried to wiggle her big toe. Sure enough it twitched. The little cat saw the movement in her slippers, sprang forward, and landed its front claws on the moving toe as if it were a mouse. The old lady gasped and instinctively pulled away her foot. To her surprise her leg moved, not far, but move it did. The little cat chased her foot, pouncing again and again as she tried to escape from him. Excited now, very daringly, she leaned forward and, watched by the cat, slowly rose from her chair. Then, shuffling more than walking, she moved towards the kitchen and poured a full saucer of milk. The little cat busied itself with the milk, purring as it drank, while the old lady tried walking a few more steps round the room.

That evening, the old lady dared to venture out of the front door and, with the aid of an old stick, hobbled two doors down the street to Mr Singh's little general store on the corner.

'It's a miracle!' the shopkeeper exclaimed on seeing her.

The old lady smiled knowingly but said it was no such thing and bought two tins of the best cat food.

But when she got home, there was no sign of the little cat and, to her dismay, it did not return that night, or the next morning. So, cautiously, she ventured a little way up the street calling for it but without success. Each day she went a little further but no one she asked had seen the little cat and by the end of the week she had walked the entire length of the village, in both directions.

A few days later it was Christmas Day and she even managed to climb the hill to the village church. After the service, when the vicar's wife asked her if she would adopt one of the kittens from the vicarage, she began to ponder on the possible truth of Mr Singh's comment and about the little cat. Was it really a miracle?

My Chestnut Tree

When I was just a tiny cat
My master bought a tree
He said it was a chestnut
And was specially for me.
I loved to climb that little tree
And play among its boughs
And always chose the highest point
To call my proud meows.

As years went by the little tree
Grew always ever bigger
But still I reached the topmost twigs
As easily as ever.
One summer day my master
Carved my name into that tree.
He said t'would live 200 years
And still belong to me!

Time passed.
The tree grew big and strong
But I grew old and lame.
My master had to lift me up

To let me see my name.
Now my poor broken body
Lies deep beneath my tree
My spirit though still climbs it
Playing happily and free.

I think my master knows I'm here
For when he stands below
He looks aloft and speaks my name
And softly calls 'hello'.
I've still to wait a little while
But then will come the day
When he and I together
Will in my chestnut play.

Please Drive Carefully

A True Story

It was the second evening of their holiday on a lovely sunny Spanish island. They had been on the beach all day, soaking up the sun and enjoying occasional dips among the waves. Now the young couple were on their way back to their apartment, in their big hire car, and looking forward to supper. The car was bigger than their own car at home and he was not yet quite adapted to driving along the narrow winding lanes on the island.

'Darling, do go more slowly! You don't know these roads!' pleaded his wife as they rounded a bend.

'We're only doing 35.'

'Yes, but they're such narrow roads.'

He smiled at her and slowed to 30.

'Better?' he asked.

'Yes, but for God's sake remember they drive on the right here!' she responded, managing a slightly forced laugh.

'Here's the turning into our road,' she said, then suddenly cried, 'Stop! Stop!'

She had seen something small running across the road and heard a bump. Whatever it was she was sure that they had hit it. She leapt out of the car and there, at the side of the road, lay a cat.

'You hit a cat!' she called to her husband as he climbed out of the driving seat and came to her. The small ginger and white cat she held was bleeding from the mouth and was quite still.

'It isn't moving, I think it must be dead,' she said sadly. It looked rather like her own cat that they had, reluctantly, left with her mother while they were on holiday, and thoughts of sadness went though her mind as she thought about the anguish this little cat's owner would have to endure because of his careless driving.

Her husband took it from her.

'Yes,' he confirmed. 'It is dead,' and handed the poor animal back to her.

'Should we take it to a vet?'

'No point, he couldn't bring it back to life, we'd better bury it.'

'But we haven't got a spade or anything.'

'Well, just leave it here then.'

'No, it will get all squashed by the next car; that's horrid,' she insisted. 'We must do something with it.' They looked at each other questioningly.

'I know,' he suggested after a pause. 'Let's put it in that big waste bin we passed at the corner.'

She seemed to half agree, it was not what she would have wanted had it been her cat, but they carried it back to the bin, a large refuse container that was emptied each morning. He climbed up the roadside bank and peered in.

'It's almost empty, give it to me.'

She passed the cat to him and he dropped it, as gently as he could, into the bin.

That was that. So, they got back into the car and tried to forget. But now he drove very slowly and his mind filled with the image of the poor little cat whose life they had ended so horribly. She was crying.

However, what they did not know was that little Gatito, for that was his name, was not dead. An hour or so later he opened his eyes to find himself at the bottom of what seemed to him a deep pit with steep slippery metal sides. He was in great pain and his legs were so bruised that he could hardly stand. He raised one paw to the wall hoping to climb out somehow but just collapsed into a heap. Still dazed and confused, he drifted into a kind of half sleep only to be awakened by voices and a bucketful of rubbish crashing down and just missing him. Gatito was terrified and tried to cry but no meow came out, just a short gush of breath. Nobody would hear him and more stuff might fall on him at any moment. He managed to drag himself painfully to the other side of the huge bin and crawl beneath an old, dirty cardboard box for protection. It started to get dark and the poor little cat had no idea what had happened to him, or how he had got there; he just knew he was hurting all over, curled himself into a little ball and cried himself to sleep.

It was a lot later that night and quite dark when an elderly couple who lived nearby were walking home from the bar and passed close to the bin.

'What was that?' asked the lady in Spanish.

'What was what, dear?' her husband responded.

'A little noise, a bit like an animal crying, listen!

They stopped walking and stood still, listening to the gentle sounds of evening.

'There! Hear that?'

'No.'

'Listen!' she persisted.

'Oh, yes! Sounds like a cat or something. Over there.'

They moved towards the almost inaudible sound coming from the bin.

'It's closer now; could it be coming from the bin?'

'I'll try and look.'

Although quite old, the man climbed, as best he could, up the bank and holding on to the bin was just able to peer in.

'Yes, it's in there, I can't see but I think it is a cat. It must have fallen in.'

There was no way that either of them could reach down or climb into the bin and they thought for a while about what they could do. They knew that lots more rubbish would be tipped into the bin next morning and, that soon after that, the big rubbish lorry would come along and everything would be tipped into the crusher and packed tightly on board. They had to do something to save the little cat and so decided to go back to the bar and get help.

'I'll go,' said the man, 'you wait here and try to stop anyone putting more rubbish in, I won't be long.'

But just as he was starting the journey back to the bar a young man appeared on a bicycle and they asked him for help.

With the aid of his cycle lamp, the lad peered into the bin and saw the little ginger and white cat at the bottom. It wasn't that easy, even for him, to climb into the bin but he did eventually manage and picked up little Gatito.

'Here he is, he looks as if he's been hit by a car,' he said, handing the cat to the lady.

She held it close in her arms, stroking and caressing it as she would her own cat.

'It looks like Senora Djano's little Gatito!' the Spanish lady exclaimed. 'He seems badly hurt. We must take him to her.'

'Can I help any more?' the lad asked, but they both felt that he had done quite enough already by climbing into the bin and getting his clothes dirty too. They thanked him and started to carry the little cat down the road to where the Senora lived. She was very upset at the sight of the bloodstained little Gatito.

'What happened?' she asked, but all they could do was tell her the story as they knew it.

Senora Djano telephoned the vet's emergency line and arranged to bring Gatito to him next morning.

There is a happy ending to this true story: Gatito was not seriously wounded. He was badly bruised and had a nasty cut on his head. The blood coming from his mouth seemed only to be from a wound where he had bitten his lip.

Next morning the young holiday couple stopped their car by the bin and, once more, the man climbed the bank and peeped in.

'It's quite empty,' he told his wife.

They hugged each other closely, tears filling both their eyes.

'Drive more carefully, please,' she begged.

Christmas Day

Of course our cats knew it was Christmas
They'd played with the things on the tree
And both had had liver for breakfast
And both would have turkey for tea.
But, for Old Tom who lived on the waste ground
Things had not been quite so good.
He'd had water thrown at him for breakfast
When he'd called at the Jones' for food.

The Johnsons had not been much better
They'd hurt him by throwing a tin
When he dared to walk up their back alley
To look for some food in their bin.
So now he sat in my garden,
With sadness and fear in his eyes,
Thinking he'd have to go hungry
With rain in the darkening skies.

I opened our door very gently,
But he jumped at the sound of the latch,
Fled to the top of the garden,
And stopped on the old cabbage patch.

Some turkey I left on the doorstep
And milk by the side of the mat.
Then closing the door, very quietly
Said a wee prayer for that cat.

The best present I had that Christmas,
When later I opened the door,
Was to find both the bowls empty
And Tom bravely asking for more.
I gave him more food in the kitchen
And cream on the rug by the fire.
And watched him lap, filling his tummy
To the brim of his heart's desire.

But I'd swear there were tears in the old cat's eyes
When he looked at the crib by the tree
Remembering that once, when a kitten,
There'd been turkey and cream for his tea.

The Broken Cat Flap

It was bad enough bringing home the empty carry-basket from the vet's but now they were home it was even worse; the house seemed so very quiet and empty. There was no little cat waiting for them in the hallway when they opened the front door, no little cat in his basket by the fireside, nor even any sign of a little cat popping in through the cat flap to greet them as there had been for all those years. The house was full of sad reminders.

On the kitchen floor was the small pool of bloodstained vomit in which they had found Thomas lying and unable to stand. He had raised his head and his eyes had pleaded with them, pitifully, for help. They had rushed him round to the vet only to be told that he had suffered a massive heart attack for which there was no hope; and so they had had to say goodbye there and then. Feeling that they had let him down, they couldn't hold back the tears.

But now, back at home, the future seemed bleak. He wanted to adopt another cat immediately to fill the gap but his wife was quite against that, feeling that no ordinary cat could possibly fill the aching void in her heart and that any attempt to replace Thomas would be so hurtful to his memory. He understood, and they sadly agreed to wait, maybe a year, before thinking, possibly, of another cat. So, to avoid having reminders all round the house, they started to clear Thomas's things away. His carry-basket and fireside bed could go up to the attic. His fireside cushion was worn and not worth keeping, but they found it too hard to throw away so put it in the garden shed. Several other items, still in good order, were packed into bags for delivery later to the local cat charity shop, and the big bag of assorted cat food, recently purchased from the local supermarket, was put aside to be taken to an elderly near neighbour for her old ginger cat, Ginge. The big problem was the cat flap in the kitchen door, which lead into the garden. It had been bought for Thomas many years ago and the catch had broken so the slightest breeze caused it to swing open allowing a draught to sweep through the kitchen. She suggested to her husband that now might be a good moment to remove the flap and he agreed, promising to do so.

Six months passed and it was now early October, when the wintry winds were once more beginning to blow through the broken cat flap.

'You promised to do something about that draught, dear,' she said, nodding towards the cat flap, while they were both in the kitchen making tea.

'Yes, I know,' he responded. 'I've looked at it several times but it's not that easy.'

Indeed, he had looked at the job and the options were limited. He could replace the cat flap with a new one that would have a working lock, but what was the point of an expensive new cat flap if they had no cat? The other options were a whole new back door or to try and remove the existing lower panel from the door and replace it, which he thought was probably beyond his limited carpentry skill. But, nevertheless, he looked at the job once more and promised his wife that he would go and get the necessary wood and ask the store to cut a panel for him of exactly the right size.

True to his word, he took careful measurements of the panel's size and the very next morning, on his way to work, he visited the local builders' merchant, selected a suitable sheet of plywood and took it along to the corner that housed the cutting service. There a notice greeted him:

OWING TO SAFETY ISSUES IT HAS BEEN NECESSARY TO SUSPEND OUR NORMAL SERVICE. WE HOPE TO REINSTATE THE SERVICE AS SOON AS POSSIBLE AND APOLOGISE FOR ANY INCONVENIENCE TO OUR CUSTOMERS

He left the store empty-handed, but then happened to drive past *Bob's Pets,* where they had often bought various little luxuries for Thomas and, amazingly, there was a parking space directly in front of the shop. Yes, they did have an identical new cat flap, which would make it very easy to fit. He checked that the lock worked and bought the new flap. After all, he hoped that his wife might soon agree to obtaining a new cat, so why fit a new door panel that would only have to be cut when a new flap was eventually needed? It all seemed suddenly to make better sense. On arriving home, he put the new flap into one of the kitchen drawers telling his wife that he would install it as soon as he could find time.

Every morning he came down to the kitchen, made their early morning tea and took it back up to the bedroom. Time had passed and it was many days after buying the new flap, on a cold November morning, that he got out of bed and came down to the kitchen as usual only to find the draught blowing furiously through the old flap. He glanced guiltily at the drawer where the new flap was still tucked away awaiting his attention. As always he filled the kettle and then went to the fridge to get out the milk; but what was that in an old cardboard box by the fridge?

'Darling!' he called. 'Come quickly!'

Thinking he had had some awful accident, his wife appeared by his side in an instant.

'Look!' he said, pointing to the box where a little cat was lying, purring loudly and feeding three tiny kittens.

'Where on earth did they come from?' she asked, not really expecting an answer. But that was the big question.

They spent much of that day asking neighbours, the local vet and even the police if they had any idea as to whom the cat might belong. They pinned notices on the lamp post outside their house, but there was no response. So, next day, as a last resort, they called the local cat sanctuary. The lady from there came round to check if the cat was microchipped but, alas, there were no clues at all as to its identity. She did, however, seem to know a lot about cats and explained to them that the mother cat had probably strayed from her home or maybe the people had moved away without her. She had probably been living wild, perhaps in some old shed, but seeking warmth for her kittens, had seen the open cat flap and come in. So many cat flaps, she said, were locked at night.

'Will you be able to keep her?' the sanctuary lady asked.

He glanced at his wife, willing her to say yes. She hesitated looking at the little cat and her kittens.

'She's very lovely isn't she? I think we could,' she responded eventually, listening to the cat's loud hypnotic purr.

'That's so kind of you,' the lady replied smiling. 'We have so many abandoned cats to look after at the moment.'

As soon as the lady left he put his arm round his wife and they watched their new cat as she washed each of her little kittens, purring loudly and glancing at them between licks. Tomasina seemed to know that she had found a new and loving home, and the man and his wife were both so happy. One thing was now certain; at last there would soon be a brand new cat flap in the kitchen door.

The moral of this story is: '*Never do today what you can put off till tomorrow*!'

<u>A Problem Solved</u>

Where shall I bury my poor dear pet?
Now that I've brought her home from the vet.
She had to be taken for one final visit
I think it was right, but you tell me, is it?
Her god, he has taken her spirit, now free,
But her poor lifeless body, he left that to me!

O, where shall I bury my poor cat's remains?
Now that, for ever, she's free of her pains.
There's a patch on my lawn where the grass is
worn bare,
I suppose I could dig a nice grave for her there.
Though I think she'd prefer to be under the rose,
But a headstone just there would entangle the hose.

My neighbour, who's of a most practical type,
Suggested I 'buck up and cut out the hype!'
He gave me a black bag to wrap her up in
And offered to put her in his wheelie bin.
With the logic of which I could but agree
Because, as he said, it's a service that's free.
But I felt that my puss-cat deserved something finer
Than ending her days in a poly bin-liner.

When he heard of my problem the vicar had said
'There's a spot in the graveyard just by the old shed
Close to the place where my dog, Tray, lies buried.
I'd say you should dig her grave there if you're
worried.'
But somehow I think that the thing she'd hate most
Would be lying so close to the vicar's dog's ghost!

Could I ask her, she'd say being food for a fox
Was better than being nailed-up in a box.
And although that is the most natural end
I just could not do that to such a good friend.
But I see lots of wood on the old bonfire patch
So the whole thing can, surely, be solved with a
match
Aided perhaps with some paraffin oil.
T'would be better than rotting away in the soil.

So I don't need to bury my poor old pet
And never again need she go to the vet.
Her body's now joined her spirit so free
And her name I have carved on her favourite tree.

(With apologies to Rev Richard Harris Barham, aka
'Thomas Ingoldsby Esquire' – *Ingoldsby Legends.*)

Christmas Matins

Lower Mossford is an unspoilt village with a beautiful church. The rector was a popular gentleman and a true traditionalist. He felt it quite unnecessary to have to translate 'thy will' to 'your will' for the congregation and so always used the original text of the Book of Common Prayer. Likewise, he thought, why insult them by using some trivial easy-reader version of the bible instead of the beautiful King James version?

This proved very popular and attracted a large congregation to the church.

Hill Farm is situated close by, and Jim, the farmer, also chairs the Church Council. Jim has a dog, but no cats of his own. There was one feral tabby cat that occasionally crossed the farm courtyard, sometimes carrying a mouse in its mouth, and from time to time the farmer's wife tried to offer it a plate of leftovers. At first the cat was too scared to approach her, but eventually it learned to trust its lady provider more and more. Nobody knew where the cat spent most of its time, but on some of the coldest winter nights it crept into Jim's old barn for shelter.

As time passed, they both grew very fond of the little tabby and, feeling it should have a name, decided to call it Bonnie.

One grey November afternoon, while looking through the kitchen window, Jim's wife noticed Bonnie cross the courtyard to the barn for the third time that day.

'It seems to be in and out of the old barn a lot,' she commented.

Jim said he'd investigate and later went over to explore the barn. He found the cat curled up on a pile of old sacks, nursing a bundle of kittens!

'Bonnie's a girl and she's got kittens,' he told his wife, with a big smile.

'Then we will have to look after her, won't we?' she said, delighted by the news. 'I'll make a nice big plate of tasty food for her.'

So it was decided that Bonnie and her kittens could remain in the barn.

All went well until one day, a couple of weeks later, Jim entered the barn to find one of his prize-winning chickens lying dead and half-eaten on the floor.

'She can't stay there,' he told his wife sadly, regretting every word as he spoke.

'I suppose not,' his wife had to agree, her eyes filling with tears. 'Perhaps we'd better arrange for the Cats Protection people to collect her; they should be able to find homes for them all.'

But when she came to collect Bonnie and the kittens, the cat lady explained that, though homes would easily be found for the kittens, finding a home for a feral cat like Bonnie would be much harder. Jim and his wife looked at each other sadly on hearing that; they so much wanted dear Bonnie to have a happy home, but away from the chickens.

It was now Advent Sunday, and at Matins the church was full and the rector had just got near to the end of the Second Collect.

'—that we, surely trusting in thy defence—' he was saying, when there was a sudden loud scream from somewhere in the congregation. Unruffled, as he always was, the rector completed the Collect before looking up.

A lady, half way back on the right-hand side of the church, was standing on her pew, still screaming, and holding her skirt up to knee height. The verger was already at her pew and the organist had also risen and was walking towards her.

'Please, calm down! What's the matter?' asked the rector, arriving quickly at the pew.

'Rats! On my leg!' she cried jumping down and running out of the church, still screaming, and followed closely by her husband.

'There was a rat,' explained one of the gentlemen near her in the row. 'It ran off.'

The rector returned to his place, apologised for the interruption, and went on to read the Third Collect.

Standing at the church door after the service and saying goodbye to the people as they left, it was farmer Jim's turn to shake hands with the rector.

'We'll have to talk about this at the next Church Council meeting,' Jim said, smiling.

The following Wednesday, item one on the agenda was indeed 'rats', and over the next half-hour several, mostly impracticable, suggestions were put forward by members of the council. At last, having waited patiently, the chairman put forward the plan he and his wife had carefully thought out for Bonnie.

'What about a church cat?' he proposed.

This resulted in a general nodding of approval from the members round the table, as it was, after all, by far the least expensive remedy that had been suggested.

So it was that, not long after her kittens had been homed, Bonnie found herself installed by Jim and the verger in a comfortable bed just off the vestry and with a plentiful supply of food. From there she was able to wander round the whole church and had access to the graveyard through a crack in the woodwork of the north door, which was used only for funerals. Over the following weeks, the verger cared lovingly for Bonnie; they soon became great friends, and many dismembered rats and mice were found in the vestry. The rector was delighted, and was able to persuade the screaming lady, and the intrepid congregation, that the church was now vermin-free and safe for their return in time for the Christmas Day service.

So now all was well; the congregation had all come back to church, the rector was delighted with the cheap solution to his problem, the verger had fallen hopelessly in love with Bonnie, the organist played *All Creatures Great and Small,* Jim and his wife were very happy with the arrangement, and the prize chickens were now safe. Best of all, Bonnie had found a perfect home.

The End

Part Two

Notes on adopting and looking after
your cat

Owning a Cat

There are so many ways that people acquire cats! Maybe you fancy an expensive pedigree variety of some kind; in which case be warned. Pedigrees, because of intensive inbreeding, can be liable to all kinds of medical problems, which are both sad and expensive, so it is extremely important to choose your breeder with great care and to ask people who have obtained cats from them if they have had any problems.

On the whole, the common *Domestic Shorthair*, or what we might call an ordinary cat, is a happier and much cheaper choice; and the choice is enormous: *Tabbies*, *Black and Whites*, *Blacks*, *Gingers and Tortoiseshells*, to mention only a few of the common varieties; and of course, the choice of a male or female. Remember that Gingers are almost always male and Tortoiseshells almost always female.

Before thinking about where to get your cat, think carefully about whether you can really look after one well for its lifetime. You might be thinking of getting a cat as better company and greater educational value than a new teddy bear, for your children. An excellent idea, but remember that, like us, cats live longer these days, many reaching 20 or more, so the children may well have obtained their university degrees and be married with their own children before the time comes for your cat to leave the planet!

Of course, the decision may not be yours! The best of all options is that some poor lost cat has found you and decided to move in. In that case, you can be sure that he has already surveyed the area, investigated alternative homes and decided it's you he wants to live with. Nokomis and Dylan both came to us just like that and we were handsomely rewarded.

Dylan — Please may I come in?

He did and he stayed.

The cost of keeping a cat

It's not just the cost of the cat itself, pedigree or otherwise, that you must think about. Cat food is expensive these days and carries VAT so costing you quite a lot. Add to that the annual visits to the vet for injections to protect your cat from various common conditions. Advisedly also, the cost of insurance to cover any major veterinary expenses, which could be well over £2,000, should your cat develop a serious illness or be involved in an accident. Comprehensive insurance is not cheap and even the best policies carry an excess, and many an additional percentage, that you will have to pay on each claim. Then, of course, what to do with your cat should you have to be away from home or wish to go on holiday. Boarding catteries are not cheap either.

Obtaining your cat

So, you have decided on an ordinary kitten, better still *two* kittens as they will be much happier together. It's best if you and your intended kittens can get to know each other before they leave their mother, so ask around. Ask the local vet or pet shop if they know someone whose cat has just had kittens, or perhaps there may be an advertisement in the local paper. Contact them as soon as possible, select your kittens and try to visit them and give them a little cuddle, as often as you can, before you eventually take them home. Kittens will bond with you much better if adopted as young as possible. Most vets will tell you to forget the old wives' tale that a kitten shouldn't leave its mother until it is at least eight weeks old; five weeks is an ideal adoption age.

Acquiring an older cat

Maybe you have decided an older cat would better suit your needs. As well as providing some poor homeless cat with a new home, adopting a stray is a kind act in itself and will help your bonding with the new arrival! As with kittens, your vet may know of someone who can no longer keep their cat. Or again, there may be an advertisement. But all the rescue centres will have a good selection and you will have no trouble finding a cat, or cats, of the right age, sex and colour. The staff will be able to tell you about the cat and advise you on its general character. Most cat charities will want to check your home to see if it's cat-friendly and safe and will need to come and inspect it. A house with no garden situated on a busy road, or perhaps a flat on the sixth floor of a tower block would be regarded as unsuitable. If you adopt, the charity will appreciate a donation; be as generous as possible – they do a splendid job for cats.

The cats arrive home

First, your new cats or kittens will explore the whole of your house and will then ask to venture into your garden. Do not think that you must keep them indoors for a number of weeks before they can have access to the garden. Once they are fully relaxed, know you well and have learned where their food is served, perhaps as soon as two or three days, it should be safe to accompany them into the garden before they have had breakfast. Mother cats usually take their kittens into the garden to learn about the outside world and how to catch their dinners at a very early age – almost as soon as they can walk.

Don't expect too much love from your kittens; love comes later. Yes, they may well find your bed is a nice warm place to sleep, and purr loudly at night, but it will be the comfort and warmth they are enjoying and probably not you – yet.

Kittens get into trouble all too frequently. I have known one get stuck under the fridge, another behind a radiator, and yet another managed to get under the floorboards and couldn't remember the way out! So check on their whereabouts regularly and listen for their cry if they do vanish. But don't panic too soon, kittens can sleep quietly for many hours in some warm dark hidden place and emerge safely at dinnertime.

Feeding your cat

Modern commercial cat foods vary not only in flavour but also in quality and you may have to try several to find one your cat really enjoys. Cats' natural diet is, of course, freshly-caught raw meat, which contains all the nutrients a cat needs, including the amino acid *taurine*. Our bodies can make taurine but cats cannot and so must be provided with it. Cooking meat destroys much of the taurine so if you decide to avoid the VAT on cat food by providing them with butchers' meat, be sure they eat it raw. Alternatively, serve them some commercial cat food as well; nearly all contain added taurine. For kittens, the best choice is a good brand of kitten food, which will contain all the vitamins and food supplements needed by a kitten and give them a better start in life. At six or nine months it will be time to start introducing them to occasional meals of, or containing, some adult food.

<u>Neutering</u>

Whether to have your cat neutered or not is always a question, unless it was adopted from a rescue centre, in which case it will already have been neutered. Male cats, unless, of course, pedigrees intended for breeding, should always be neutered. Un-neutered male cats can be quite wild and difficult to domesticate. They will also constantly mark their territory by spraying, including the inside of your house. As regards non-pedigree female cats, the advice you will generally receive will be to have them neutered as early as possible. However, kittens are a wonderful experience and a joy, particularly for young children. So consider perhaps letting her have one litter before neutering.

Having kittens should always be delayed until the cat is at least one year, and preferably eighteen months old. So you will either have to accomplish the impossible task of keeping her indoors when on heat, or arrange with your vet for her to have injections to delay the onset of the mating urge. Don't be surprised, though, if your vet advises very strongly against kittens – if every female cat was allowed to have them, there would be an awful lot around! But it is your decision and not the vet's.

Choosing a vet

Your choice of vet is another thing you will have to think about. These days, just as do our human hospitals, veterinary establishments need expensive equipment. Most vets will have their own x-ray equipment, though it may in some cases be old and primitive. Only the larger establishments, which have several vets on their staff, and probably several branches, will usually be able to afford, and be fully competent with, modern diagnostic equipment such as ultrasound and even MRI scanners. Their operating theatres, too, will be more fully equipped, some may even have equipment to perform *key-hole surgery* and many will have a full-time night nurse to provide 24-hour care for any animals who may have to stay in hospital overnight.

On the other hand, you may prefer the one-vet establishment where you and your cats will more quickly become known to the vet and will often get a more personal approach. The surgery could be in the vet's own home and thus your cat could have 24-hour cover from him. Smaller establishments are often less expensive too. As always, ask some of your cat-owning friends which vets they use, and why.

Choosing a boarding cattery

You will be more relaxed and enjoy your holiday better if you know your cats are being well looked after and are happy in their holiday accommodation. So think about which local cattery you will use and book well in advance of your holiday, as the best catteries often get booked up very early.

It's always a good idea to start by asking your friends who have cats which cattery they use and if they and their cats are happy about it. Ask your vet too, but many prefer not to advise on catteries for professional reasons. The reception staff may, however, be able to. When you do have a place in mind, go and see it yourself. Look around generally before you go in and ask yourself if you feel satisfied with the area. Does it look safe? Are there any industrial sites nearby that might emit smoke or fumes of some kind? Is the establishment well kept and do they also board dogs? If you don't have a dog at home, constant barking could worry your cats, so choose an establishment that does not accommodate dogs.

Are its gardens in good order and is the property in good condition? Maybe it's not obviously relevant but little details like that can tell you a lot about the owners and the state of their finances. Note their attitude and remember that some catteries are run by people who really love cats, others by people who just want to make some money.

Try not to make an appointment to view, but just turn up – if they won't show you round immediately you should wonder why. Could they want to tidy or clean up some messes before showing you round? When you do get in, try to see all the pens, which may, in a big cattery, be divided between several houses and be of different sizes, standards of comfort and security.

Check that there is a scratching post in each pen and, as cats love to be high up, that there are high shelves where they can sit, and also an enclosed cabin where they can hide if they so choose. Of course, heating arrangements and air conditioning should be discussed also.

Cleanliness is important. Cats are, by nature, clean animals and appreciate a clean environment. Make sure the feeding bowls are clean and not covered with flyblow and that the water bowls look full and fresh. Food bowls should be removed, whether empty or not, after the cats have had access to them for a reasonable time. Does the establishment have a dishwasher and refrigerator?

Also, and very importantly, how do the cats seem? Do they look happy? Are any purring and coming to their door to talk to you as you pass by during your inspection? Or do they run away and hide as if afraid of the cattery people, suggesting perhaps that they are not lovingly cared for.

If you have any slight doubts about how the cattery is run, say that you have a friend who lives close by and knows your cats, and ask if they could pop in now and again to see them? If the management insists that they give them notice of such a visit, ask yourself why? Could it be that, as some catteries do, your cat will be moved from the deluxe pen you saw her settled into, to some less comfortable pen elsewhere as soon as your back is turned? Regrettably such things do happen!

Finally, in the UK all Animal Boarding Establishments, however small, need to be licensed by the Local Authority. The licence should be conspicuously displayed on the premises; if you can't see it, ask to.

The cat-sitter option

Now think about your cats. Do they really need to go to a cattery at all? Might it be better for them to stay at home and be looked after by a cat-sitter? Young cats and kittens are always quite happy first-timers at a cattery; they find lots to explore, new experiences are welcome to them and they will get an early opportunity to learn about catteries and the all-important point: that you will be coming back to pick them up and take them home. For that reason I often advise people to bring first-timers in for a one or two night stay a few days before they are brought in for their real and longer stay.

Older cats, six or eight years old, may find cattery life very frightening if they have not been before, but if the stay is not for more than a couple of weeks, they will settle eventually and understand. Very old cats, 13 years and older who have never been to a cattery, will be most unhappy. They may not eat for a week and simply hide in their refuge all the time. They will, however, nearly always survive but stress can, for example in a cat with a serious existing heart problem, provoke a fatal heart attack!

Almost all cats would prefer to be looked after at home than have to go to a cattery but I have met exceptions. One or two of our regular visitors always go and hide in their cabins the moment they hear their owners approaching on going-home day. They would obviously rather stay with us! A cat sitter will normally come to your home once, or more usually twice a day to feed your cat and, if required, clean and refill the litter tray. Many will also help to make the house seem occupied by bringing in the post, putting the dustbins out for collection and watering your houseplants. It's quite a good idea to use both options, a cat-sitter for absences of only a few days and a cattery for longer times.

Whether you choose a cattery or cat-sitter, try always to use the same one. Cats have excellent memories. Very often, cats coming to stay with us trot along the cattery corridor on arrival and stop outside the pen they were in on their last visit, even if that was over a year before. Likewise they recognise and are glad to greet their regular cat-sitting friend.

When you come home from your holiday, you can be sure your feline friends will tell you how things have been while you were away. Take heed of their report.

In Loving Memory
of
Alfie
killed by a car just as this book went to press,
and to whom the book is dedicated.